Botanical
Flower Mandalas
coloring book
Volume 1

Illustrated by
Pamela Duarte

Botanical Flower Mandalas Coloring Book, Volume 1
©2019 Pamela Duarte

All rights reserved. No part of this book may be reproduced or transmitted by any form or by any means, electronic or mechanical, including photocopy, recording, or any information storage or retrieval system, without prior written consent from the author.

I have created coloring books for other clients in my career as a professional illustrator but for a long time have wanted to illustrate a book in which I could create the subject matter on my own. I love flowers and the natural world and so chose that as the inspiration for this book. If you love flowers too, please collaborate with me!

This book is dedicated to 3 strong women:

My Mother who has always been supportive of my goals,
My Grandmother who taught me to appreciate beauty,
and to
Carolee Bingham who loved to color mandalas
& who inspired this book.

This is a new addition of "Flower Mandalas, Vol. 1" published in 2015. The art has been resized and, in some cases, revised and each design has been printed twice.

The pages of this book are suitable for colored pencils, markers, and a variety of other media. They are only printed on one side and to help prevent bleed through, please place a blank sheet of paper between the pages when coloring.

African Corn Lily
Ixia Longituba

African Corn Lily
Ixia Longituba

African Ice Plant
Cephalopyllum Pillansii

African Ice Plant
Cephalopyllum Pillansii

Angel's Trumpet
Brugmansia

Angel's Trumpet

Brugmansia

Bougainvillea
Bougainvillea glabra

Bougainvillea
Bougainvillea glabra

Clivia
Amaryllidaceae

Clivia
Amaryllidaceae

Cyclamen
Primulaceae

Cyclamen
Primulaceae

Cymbidium Orchid
Orchidaceae

Cymbidium Orchid
Orchidaceae

Dahlia
Asteraceae

Dahlia
Asteraceae

Forest Lily
Veltheimia Bracteata

Forest Lily
Veltheimia Bracteata

Gazania
Gazania Splendens

Gazania
Gazania Splendens

Harlequin Flower
Spraxix Elegans

Harlequin Flower
Spraxix Elegans

Hibiscus
Hibisceae

Hibiscus
Hibisceae

Hyacinth
Hyacinthus

Hyacinth
Hyacinthus

Hydrangea
Hydrangeaceae

Hydrangea
Hydrangeaceae

Knight's Star Lily
Hippeastrum

Knight's Star Lily

Hippeastrum

Lotus
Nelumbo nucifera

Lotus
Nelumbo nucifera

Lupine
Lupinus

Lupine
Lupinus

Magnolia
Magnoliaceae

Magnolia
Magnoliaceae

Marguerite Daisy
Argyranthemum frutescens

Marguerite Daisy
Argyranthemum frutescens

Moon Flower
Ipomoea

Moon Flower
Ipomoea

Moraea
Iridaceae

Moraea
Iridaceae

Daffodil
Narcissus

Daffodil
Narcissus

Nasturtium
Tropaeolum

Nasturtium
Tropaeolum

Passion Flower
Passifloraceae

Passion Flower
Passifloraceae

Peruvian Lily
Alstroemeria

Peruvian Lily
Alstroemeria

Rose
Rosaceae

Rose
Rosaceae

Sunflower
Helianthus

Sunflower
Helianthus

Tulip
Tulipa

Tulip
Tulipa

Waterlily
Nymphaea

Waterlily
Nymphaea

Zinnia
Zinnia Elegans

Zinnia
Zinnia Elegans

About The Artist

Pamela Duarte received a BFA from Art Center College of Design. After graduation she worked as a fashion illustrator and then segued into fashion dolls. She has worked on projects for many companies including Mattel Toys where she has illustrated Barbie and other products. She has also designed for toy companies in Hong Kong.

She loves to travel and has lived in Los Angeles, New York, and Bali. She currently lives in the peaceful Ojai Valley.

Other books by this Artist:
Botanical Flower Mandalas Coloring Book, Volume 2
Flower Patterns Coloring Books, Volume 1 & 2
Flowers & Fashion Coloring Book
Vivid Beauty Coloring Book

These illustrations are for personal use only.

www.ingramcontent.com/pod-product-compliance
Lightning Source LLC
Chambersburg PA
CBHW080920170526
45158CB00008B/2181